First World War
and Army of Occupation
War Diary
France, Belgium and Germany

15 DIVISION
46 Infantry Brigade,
Brigade Trench Mortar Battery
9 November 1915 - 31 August 1916

WO95/1954/4

The Naval & Military Press Ltd
www.nmarchive.com
Published in association with The National Archives

Published by

The Naval & Military Press Ltd

Unit 10 Ridgewood Industrial Park,

Uckfield, East Sussex,

TN22 5QE England

Tel: +44 (0) 1825 749494

www.naval-military-press.com

www.nmarchive.com

This diary has been reprinted in facsimile from the original. Any imperfections are inevitably reproduced and the quality may fall short of modern type and cartographic standards.

© **Crown Copyright**
Images reproduced by permission of The National Archives, London, England, 2015.

Contents

Document type	Place/Title	Date From	Date To
Heading	WO95/1954/4		
Heading	15 Div 46 Bde 46 Trench Mortar Bty 1915 Nov To 1916 Aug. 1652		
War Diary	Lindenhock	12/11/1915	13/11/1915
War Diary	Berthen	09/11/1915	09/11/1915
War Diary	Lindenhock	10/11/1915	11/11/1915
War Diary	Wulverghem	14/11/1915	01/01/1916
Heading	War Diary Of 46th Trench Mortar Battery 1-7-16 To 31-7-16 (Volume)		
Miscellaneous	46th Inf. Bde. No. S.C/38/3	29/08/1916	29/08/1916
War Diary	Hulluch Sector	01/07/1916	01/07/1916
War Diary	Trenches	02/07/1916	13/07/1916
War Diary	Gosnay 15th Div. School	14/07/1916	20/07/1916
War Diary	Marles Les Mines	21/07/1916	21/07/1916
War Diary	Heuchin.	22/07/1916	25/07/1916
War Diary	Croisette.	26/07/1916	26/07/1916
War Diary	Chateau de Beauvoir	27/07/1916	27/07/1916
War Diary	Berneuil (Somme)	28/07/1916	30/07/1916
War Diary	Flesselles (Somme)	31/07/1916	31/07/1916
Heading	46th Brigade. 15th Division. 46th Light Trench Mortar Battery August 1916		
War Diary	Flesselles	01/08/1916	03/08/1916
War Diary	Molliens au Bois	03/08/1916	03/08/1916
War Diary	Franvillers	04/08/1916	05/08/1916
War Diary	Trenches East Of Albert.	06/08/1916	19/08/1916
War Diary	Bois Noir. East of Albert	20/08/1916	26/08/1916
War Diary	Trenches East Of Albert	27/08/1916	31/08/1916

Woas/lash/4

~~2 Army Corps~~

15 DIV 46 Bde

46

TRENCH MORTAR
BTY

1915 NOV to 1916 AUG

1652

WAR DIARY
or
INTELLIGENCE SUMMARY

Army Form. C. 2118

Sheet No. 2.

(Erase heading not required.)

#6 th Trench Mortar Battery

Place	Date	Hour	Summary of Events and Information	Remarks and references to Appendices
LINDENHOEK	Nov 1915 12		The left half Battery having completed the operation it was specially detailed for to the satisfaction of the G.O.C. 6th Canadian Infantry Brigade, the Mortars were withdrawn from the trenches and arrangements made for the move of the half Battery to the 1st Canadian Division.	
"	13		Rained heavily, which made the carrying of the Mortars most difficult, it was impossible to use the wheels owing to the deepness of the mud, eventually all stores were loaded on transport at LINDENHOEK and the half Battery proceeded to billets near WULVERGHEM where it joined the left half Battery.	

F. Thompson Lieut
O.C. 6 T.M. Batt
CANADIAN

Army Form. C. 2118

WAR DIARY
Sheet No. 1.
or
INTELLIGENCE SUMMARY

(Erase heading not required.)

46th Trench Mortar Battery.

Place	Date	Hour	Summary of Events and Information	Remarks and references to Appendices
Bertha	Nov 15 9	9 a.m.	1st Survey Rept. A 2nd Lieut. J. Thompson took over command of the Battery which had been organised and trained at the Trench Mortar School 2nd Army. The Battery was equipped with (4) four two inch Trench Mortars. On completion of the Takeover, the left half Battery proceeded by Motor lorry to join the 1st Canadian Division and was attached to the 1st Canadian Infantry Brigade. The left half Battery went into billets near WULVERGHEM. The right half Battery having been ordered to join the 2nd the 2nd Canadian Division proceeded by motor lorry to LINDENHOEK where horse transport was provided to convey the half Battery to TEA FARM, Headquarters of the 5th & 6th Canadian Infantry, to whom the half Battery was attached. Spent the night at the Farm.	(initials)
LINDENHOEK	10	8 a.m.	Proceeded to Trenches to reconnoitre and select positions for emplacements with a view to dealing with certain strong points in the enemy lines. These points were too close to our Trenches to be dealt with effectively by our artillery.	
		1.30 p.m.	Commenced digging emplacements.	
	11	8 a.m.	Completed emplacements and placed two Mortars in position.	
" "		3 p.m.	Commenced firing on MUSKRAT MOUND. This was a particularly strong point which was thought to be constructed of cement and iron but this is not the case, as the explosion of one shell placed in round went through the top of the position. Huge timbers and sandbags were blown into the air, after our round exploded two other explosions occurred throwing up much smoke. It obviously blew up a bomb store. Twenty four rounds were fired, seventeen were effective and practically destroyed the position. About 6 p.m. hostile troops were observed attempting to repair the damage, a machine gun was promptly turned on to them. Our Artillery cooperated by bombarding the enemy's positions at intervals during the afternoon.	

Army Form. C. 2118

WAR DIARY
Sheet No 3.
or
INTELLIGENCE SUMMARY

(Erase heading not required.) 46th Trench Mortar Battery

Instructions regarding War Diaries and Intelligence Summaries are contained in F. S. Regs., Part II. and the Staff Manual respectively. Title Pages will be prepared in manuscript.

Place	Date	Hour	Summary of Events and Information	Remarks and references to Appendices
WULVERGHEM	Nov. 15 14		Reconnoitred position occupied by 1st Canadian Infantry Brigade, found some difficulty in selecting suitable positions for emplacements. The sector is very open and is overlooked by Messines. Left section went into the trenches.	
"	15		Commenced construction of emplacements. Visited Headquarters, 2nd Canadian Divisional Artillery and obtained maps of sector.	
"	16		Continued construction of emplacements, unable to dig deeper than 3ft owing to drainage difficulties.	
"	17		Found it necessary to revet sides of emplacements with timbers driven into bottom of emplacement about a foot. The tops of the timbers were anchored to strong pickets. The timber used was salvaged from shell trenches which had caved in as soon as heavy rains set in, owing to not being properly revetted.	
"	18		Placed mortar in position, worked on drainage of emplacement.	
"	19		Worked on improvements in advanced billet, erected sandbag wall on exposed side of the building, put in doors and windows and improved the sanitary arrangements. Capt. Sir John Keane, Commandant of the French Mortar Brigade, 2nd Army visited the Battery.	
"	20		Received supply of stores from Royal Engineers, commenced construction of bomb stores. The weather during the past week was cold with some rain and frost.	

T Johnston Lieut
O.C. 46th Trench Mortar Battery

Army Form. C. 2118

WAR DIARY
or
INTELLIGENCE SUMMARY

(Erase heading not required.) 46th Trench Mortar Battery.

Sheet No. 4.

Place	Date	Hour	Summary of Events and Information	Remarks and references to Appendices
WULVERGHEM	Nov 15. 21	11 am	Right Section relieved Left Section in the trenches. Both sides shelling heavily during the afternoon. Weather mild with some frost. Left Section fired six rounds during the afternoon. Continued construction of bomb store.	
	22		Completed bomb store. Thick fog throughout the day. Received 30 bombs.	
	23		Commenced dugout. Thick fog. Front emplacements quiet.	
	24		Continued dugout. Our artillery heavily bombarded enemy positions throughout the day, to which the hostile artillery replied somewhat feebly.	
	25		Continued dugout and improved drainage of emplacement. Received supply of material from Royal Engineers for construction of emplacements and dugouts.	
	26		Commenced construction of new emplacement. Cold with some snow at intervals throughout the day.	
	27		Continued emplacement and placed mortar in position. A little shelling by both sides during the morning, remainder of day quiet.	

H.J. Thompson Lieut
O.C. 46th Trench Mortar Battery.

Army Form. C. 2118

WAR DIARY
or
INTELLIGENCE SUMMARY
(Erase heading not required.)

No 6 Canadian Mortar Battery

Instructions regarding War Diaries and Intelligence Summaries are contained in F.S. Regs., Part II. and the Staff Manual respectively. Title Pages will be prepared in manuscript.

Place	Date	Hour	Summary of Events and Information	Remarks and references to Appendices
WULVERGHEM	Nov 15 28	11 a.m.	Left section relieved right section in the trenches. Lecture by O.C. Battery on following subjects:— 1. Duties of all ranks in attack and defence. 2. Prevention of frozen feet. 3. General sanitary. 4. Orders recently issued affecting the Battery, read and explained.	
"	"	2 p.m.	Continued construction of emplacements.	
"	29	—	Reconnoitred new position of line recently taken over by 1st Canadian Infantry Brigade, and commenced construction of emplacements.	
"	30		Revetted emplacements and commenced construction of tombstones. Lieut Rogers took over command of Trench Mortar Batteries 1st Canadian Division.	
"	Dec 15 1.		Continued construction of tombstones. Sketch showing emplacements and ground covered by each mortar forwarded to G.O.C. 1st Canadian Infantry Brigade. German artillery commenced shelling our trenches about 2 p.m. and continued throughout the afternoon, our artillery replied vigorously.	
"	2		Improved drainage of emplacements.	
"	3		Commenced dugout for detachment on lines similar to one recently constructed, which has successfully resisted the recent heavy rains.	
"	4		Continued construction of dugout. Inspection of kits of right section by O.C. Battery.	

F.F. Thompson Lieut
O.C. No 6th T.M. Battery.

Army Form. C. 2118

WAR DIARY
or
INTELLIGENCE SUMMARY Sheet No. 6

(Erase heading not required.)

Instructions regarding War Diaries and Intelligence Summaries are contained in F. S. Regs., Part II. and the Staff Manual respectively. Title Pages will be prepared in manuscript.

Place	Date	Hour	Summary of Events and Information	Remarks and references to Appendices
WULVERGHEM	Dec 15. 5	11 a.m.	Right Section relieved left section in the Trenches. Lecture by O.C. Battery on discipline. Field Telephone were run from emplacement to fire Trench, with a view to registering at first opportunity.	
"	6	—	Rained heavily during the morning. Worked on improvement of emplacements during the afternoon. Enemy shelled our trenches about 9 p.m. A small high explosive shell landed on the top of the dugout occupied by "A" Subsection one man was wounded, the remainder of the detachment were in the dugout and owed their escape to the fact that the dugout was substantially built" and had at least two feet of earth on the roof.	
"	7	—	Our artillery shelled the enemy's trenches during the afternoon, advantage was taken of this opportunity to register on points in enemy's front line.	
"	8	—	Received supply of stores from the Royal Engineers and commenced construction of another bomb store. Interviewed the officers commanding the Battalions in the trenches on this front, and discussed probable operations for tomorrow.	
"	9	—	Rained heavily all day which made it impossible to carry through scheme of operations arranged yesterday. Fired 3 bombs at dusk on trenches previously registered.	
"	10	—	At the request of the G.O.C. 1st Canadian Infantry commenced construction of a defensive emplacement to cover two of our own trenches in the event of a surprise attack.	
"	11	—	Rained all day. Fired 4 Bombs into enemy's support trench. Emplacements are still free from water in spite of the recent exceptionally heavy rains and the foundations put in for the beds remain solid. The ammunition is giving better results, have had no "blind" rounds during the past week.	

F.M.Thompson Lieut
O.C. 4 6th Trench Mortar Battery,

Army Form. C. 2118

Sheet No 7.

16th French Mortar Battery

WAR DIARY
or
INTELLIGENCE SUMMARY
(Erase heading not required.)

Instructions regarding War Diaries and Intelligence Summaries are contained in F. S. Regs., Part II. and the Staff Manual respectively. Title Pages will be prepared in manuscript.

Place	Date	Hour	Summary of Events and Information	Remarks and references to Appendices
WULVERGHEM	Dec/15 12	—	Left Section relieved Right Section in the trenches. Handed over 1.2" French mortar complete with stores to 11th French Mortar Battery.	
"	13	—	Continued work on defensive emplacement, salvaged a considerable amount of timber and corrugated iron from fallen in dugouts to complete this work.	
		4 P.M.	Fired two bombs into "Factory Farm" which demolished part of a building. Three more bombs were fired into the trenches near Factory Farm with good results. This effectively stopped the sniping from the direction of the farm which had been annoying our infantry.	
"	14	4-15 p.m.	Fired four bombs into enemy trenches South of MUSKRAT MOUND, which smashed the parapet in one place and damaged his trenches considerably in others.	
"	15	3.30 p.m.	Fired seven bombs into enemy's support trenches in rear of MUSKRAT MOUND. Destroyed what was believed to be a company Headquarters also two other dugouts. An Officer of the 2nd Canadian Infantry reported that he saw eight wounded Germans leaving the trenches, some of them were on stretchers.	
"	16	—	Received 50 bombs from 1st CDAG and stores from French Mortar Brigade. Worked on improvements of emplacements. At request of Infantry did not fire owing to relief taking place.	
"	17	"	Very misty all day, unable to see hostile trenches. Situation very quiet.	
"	18	"	Worked on defensive emplacement, completed bomb store and commenced dugout for detachment. The situation during the past week has been normal, weather fair.	

T/Thornton Lieut
O.C. 16th French Mortar Battery.

19/12/15

Army Form. C. 2118

Sheet No. 8.

WAR DIARY
or
INTELLIGENCE SUMMARY

46th Medium Trench Mortar Battery

(Erase heading not required.)

Instructions regarding War Diaries and Intelligence Summaries are contained in F. S. Regs., Part II. and the Staff Manual respectively. Title Pages will be prepared in manuscript.

Place	Date	Hour	Summary of Events and Information	Remarks and references to Appendices
WULVERGHEM	Dec 15/19	11 am	Right Section relieved Left Section in the Trenches.	
"	20	—	Continued work on defensive emplacement.	
"	21	—	Rained heavily all day. Situation otherwise quiet.	
"	22	3-3.30 pm	Fired 11 bombs into enemy support and fire trenches. After 3 bombs had been fired into his fire trench, a party of the enemy were observed digging, apparently attempting to rescue some of their comrades who had been buried. 2 bombs were then fired there for air bursts, digging stopped immediately.	
"	23	3-5 pm	Fired 10 bombs at selected points in enemy fire trench with good results. Our artillery shelled enemy positions at the same time. The enemy retaliated with a number of small high explosive shells, but failed to find our position, by coming pretty near for a brief period after each salvo he sent over, he was probably led to believe he had found us, as he continued to shell the same spot although his shells were dropping harmlessly in a field some two hundred yards from our position.	
"	24	—	Received 50 bombs.	
"	25	—	Took bombs along tramway to the trenches.	

A. Thompson Lieut
O.C. 46th Trench Mortar Battery.

Army Form. C. 2118

WAR DIARY
or
INTELLIGENCE SUMMARY
(Erase heading not required.)

Sheet No. 9.

46th Trench Mortar Battery

Place	Date	Hour	Summary of Events and Information	Remarks and references to Appendices
WULVERGHEM	Dec 15 26	11 a.m.	Left Section relieved Right Section in the Trenches.	
"	27	—	Our artillery shelled enemy positions during the afternoon, the Battery joined in the bombardment & fired ten bombs into his front line which damaged his trenches considerably. Situation quiet.	
"	28	12 noon to 1.8 p.m.	Fired five bombs into enemy's front trench. Destroyed a dugout which occupied a prominent position. Our artillery shelled enemy trenches at same hour.	
"	29	—	Promoted front held by 3rd Canadian Infantry Brigade with a view to placing one or two mortars on this front as requested by the G.O.C.	
"	30	—	Intermittent shelling by both sides throughout the day.	
"	31	—	WULVERGHEM was shelled during the afternoon, otherwise quiet.	
"	Jan '16 1	4 p.m.	Demolished a suspicious looking structure in enemy's front trench, it was found to be knocked. Fired six bombs. The weather was fine during the first half of the past week, the latter half wet with strong winds.	

F.F.Thompson Lieut
O.C. 46th Trench Mortar Battery.

2/1/16

Compendium

War Diary
of
4th Trench Mortar Battery

1-7-16 To 31-7-16.

(Volume).

Headquarters,
   15th Division.

46th Inf. Bde.
No. S.C/38/

Reference 15th Division No. A/38/15
dated 24th August, 1916.

Herewith War Diary of 46th T.M. Battery
for the month of July.

Brigade H.Q.

29th Aug. 1916.

Captain,
   Staff Captain, for
      Brig. Gen.,
Commdg. 46th Inf. Bde.

PAGE ONE

Army Form C. 2118.

Instructions regarding War Diaries and Intelligence Summaries are contained in F.S. Regs., Part II. and the Staff Manual respectively. Title pages will be prepared in manuscript.

WAR DIARY
of 46th Trench Mortar Battery
~~INTELLIGENCE SUMMARY~~ 46th Brigade

(Erase heading not required.)

Place	Date	Hour	Summary of Events and Information	Remarks and references to Appendices
Hulluch Sector Trenches	July 1916 1st		Normal trench warfare	Annex
	2nd 3rd		Ditto	Annex
Ditto	4th	12 midnight	2nd Highland artillery in trenches at 12 midnight into enemy trenches in front of Hulluch. Fired 998 rds. Stokes 3" ammunition	Annex
Ditto	5th 6th		Normal trench warfare	Annex
Ditto	7th			Annex
Ditto	8th			Annex
Ditto	9th 10th 11th 12th 13th		Normal trench warfare	Annex Annex
Ditto	13th	3 p.m.	45th Trench Mortar Bty. 45th Brigade relieved 46th T.M.Bty. 46th Brigade	Annex
Gosnay 15th DW School	14th 15th 16th 17th		Starting "B" course of instruction from 4th Brigade. Carrying on course of instruction in light trench mortars - Stokes Mortar.	Annex Annex Annex
Ditto	18th			Annex
Ditto	19th	2 midnight	46th T.M.Bty. firing Stokes 3" mortars for use in Hulluch Section of trenches for that night	Annex
Ditto	20th		End of course in trench mortars	Annex
Marles les Mines	21st	10 AM-12 noon	Marched to Marles les Mines alongwith 46th Brigade	Annex
Menchin	22nd	6 AM-3 PM	Marched from Marles les Mines to Menchin with 46th Brigade	Annex
	23rd 24th 25th		At Menchin	Annex

PAGE TWO.

WAR DIARY

INTELLIGENCE SUMMARY

Army Form C. 2118.

Instructions regarding War Diaries and Intelligence Summaries are contained in F. S. Regs., Part II. and the Staff Manual respectively. Title pages will be prepared in manuscript.

(Erase heading not required.)

Place	Date	Hour	Summary of Events and Information	Remarks and references to Appendices
	July 1916.			
Crisette	26th	6.21 AM 6.130 PM	Marched with 46th Brigade from Heuchin to Crisette	Anex
Château de Beauvoir	27th	8 AM to 2 PM	(Marched with 46th Brigade from Crisette to Château de Beauvoir.	Anex
Berneuil (Somme)	28th	4.50 AM 12.15 PM	Marched from Château de Beauvoir to Berneuil (Somme) with 46th Brigade	Anex
	29th		At Berneuil (Somme)	Anex
	30th			Anex
Flesselles (Somme)	31st	4.45 AM 6.30 PM	Marched with 46th Brigade from Berneuil to Flesselles	Anex

[signature]
Lt Col
OC Battalion

46th Brigade.
15th Division.

46th LIGHT TRENCH MORTAR BATTERY

AUGUST 1 9 1 6

Secret and Confidential

PAGE ONE. WAR DIARY of 4th Trench Mortar Battery, 46th Brigade.

Army Form C. 2118.

INTELLIGENCE SUMMARY.

AUGUST 1916.

(Erase heading not required.)

Instructions regarding War Diaries and Intelligence Summaries are contained in F.S. Regs., Part II. and the Staff Manual respectively. Title pages will be prepared in manuscript.

Place	Date	Hour	Summary of Events and Information	Remarks and references to Appendices
Flesselles	August 1916. 1st 2nd and 3rd		Resting at Flesselles. Received 46th Brigade Operation Order No. 79 on 3rd.	R.W.C.
Mollienaux Bois	4th	4 AM.	Left Flesselles at 4 AM & marched via Villers Bocage to Mollienaubois.	Ympc.
Franvillers	5th	4.45 PM	Left M— aux B. at 4.45 PM & marched via Montigny and Bethencourt to Franvillers. Received 46th Brigade O.O. No. 80.	Ympc.
Trenches east of Mallart.	6th	7 AM	Left Franvillers at 7 AM, & marched via Allart to Trenches and relieved 70th T.M. Bty, 70th Brigade, 23rd Div, 46th Bde. O.O. No. 82 received. Fired 120 rds. S. Stokes 3" Amm.	Ympc.
Do.	7th		In Trenches. Received 46th Bde O.O. N. 83. Fired 252 rds. Pte E Keen wounded in leg, shell.	Xmpc.
Do.	8th		In Trenches. Fired 284 rds, assisted 112th Bde to attack on right. L/Cpl J Brown No. 14924 7/8 KOSB's wounded Eighteye	Ympc.
Do.	9th		In Trenches. Fired NIL. No. 18403 Pte J Miller, 10th S.R. Killed by shell. No. 1267 Pte A Rubenstein wounded slightly	Ympc.
Do.	10th		In Trenches. Fired 238 rds.	Ympc.
Do.	11th		In Trenches. Fired 329 rds. 2nd Lt. J M Ferguson 10th S.R. gassick shellshock.	R.W.C.
Do.	12th		In Trenches. Fired 560 rds assisting 46th Bde attack on Intermediate LINE. 18474 L/Cpl J Lockerbie 7/8th K.O.S.B. wounded arm; died of wounds next day by shell in head. 18312 Pte E Douglas 7/8 K.O.S.B. wounded — shellshock.	Ympc.
Do.	13th		In Trenches. Fired 161 rds. Received 46 Bde O.O. No. 85. 4301 Pte A Turner 12th H.L. wounded— slightly.	Ympc.
Do.	14th		In Trenches. Fired 433 rds S assisting day bombing attack of 46th Bde on Intermediate LINE. 8071 Sgt W Graham 10th S.R. killed shell. 20618 Pte W Barton 10th S.R. wounded — shellshock. 19826 Pte. A. McNeill 10/11 H.L. wounded back, shell. 14993 Pte A Naylor 7/8 K.O.S.B. wounded.	Ympc.

2353 Wt. W.2544/1454 700,000 5/15 D. D. & L. A.D.S.S./Forms/C. 2118.

Secret and Confidential

PAGE TWO.

WAR DIARY of 46th Trench Mortar Battery, 46th Bde.

INTELLIGENCE SUMMARY.

AUGUST 1916.

Army Form C. 2118.

(Erase heading not required.)

Place	Date	Hour	Summary of Events and Information	Remarks and references to Appendices
Trenches east of Pozières	1916 August 15th		In trenches: fired 29 rds: Bayt m'men join batty: Pte. Armstrong/10.S.R. goes sick.	Annex.
Do.	16th		In trenches: fired 60 rds: Received 46th Bde O.O.No. 86: Pte Nath, goes sick.	Annex.
Do.	17th		In trenches: fired 343 rds: accounted 44th Bde on relief tr attach Switch LINE: 22019/Pte W. Ferguson 7/8th K.O.S.B. killed by shell.	Annex. Annex.
Do.	18th		In trenches: fired 12 rds: Received 46th Bde O.O.No.88.	Annex.
Do.	19th 6AM–5DAM		Relieved by 45th T.M.Bty. 45th Bde. Proceeded by march to Bois Noir, east of Albert, via Becourt to bivouac. One M.G. and one man of gun front deserted.	Annex.
Bois Noir, east of Albert	20th 21st 22nd 23rd 24th 25th 26th		Resting at Bois Noir near Albert. Battery attending bomb practice, 2 Brigade school from 21st to 25th: Bde. sports final. Fired: 2nd Lt. W.W. Myles 10th S.R. joins battery, vice 2nd Lt. J.M. Ferguson 10 S.R. evacuated to all ranks. 23rd Nine men now join town hospital. 24th Received 46 Bde O.O. No.89: 14734 Pte. J. Clift 7/8th/10.S.R. evacuated sick. 27th Received 46th Bde Athmeil. Sure no. 11. 26th 14734 Pte. J. Clift 7/8th 10 S.B. evacuated sick.	Annex. Annex.
Trenches east of Albert	27th 6AM–12 Noon		6 AM Marched to trench east of Albert & relieved 37th TM Bty 3rd Bde 1st Div. Fired NIL.	Annex.
Do.	28th		In trenches: fired 40 rds: Received 46th Bde C.O.No. 90.	Annex. Annex
Do.	29th		In trenches: fired 50 rds: Received 46th Bde O.O.No. 91.	Annex
Do.	30th		In trenches: fired 45 rds: No.20971/Pte. J. Campbell.10.S.R. wounded by rifle shell.	Annex
Do.	31st		7/8th K.O.S.B. Wounded arm shrapnel. 1/3883 Pte. W. Craven	Annex.

[signed] Capt. Mortar Battery
O.C. 46th Trench Mortar Battery

www.ingramcontent.com/pod-product-compliance
Lightning Source LLC
Chambersburg PA
CBHW081509160426

43193CB00014B/2626